Eternal
LIFE

Andrew Wommack

Published by Andrew Wommack Ministries, Inc.
Woodland Park, CO 80863
awmi.net

ISBN 978-1-59548-463-5

For Worldwide Distribution, Printed in the USA

2 3 4 5 / 26 25 24 23

Contents

The Purpose of Salvation 1

What Is Eternal Life? 4

Experience Trumps an Argument 6

The Wrong Message 10

Eternal Life Changes Everything 13

Better to Be with the Lord 19

The Effects of Eternal Life: Praise 21

Counting All Things Loss 24

Knowing God 27

Ministering to the Lord 30

Blessing the Lord 31

Enter Eternal Life with God 34

Receive Jesus as Your Savior 37

Receive the Holy Spirit 39

Call for Prayer 42

About the Author 43

If I only had one s
tell you about eter

it? I already know about that. But I really believe very few of us really understand what the Bible means by "eternal life." It's much more than just living forever. It is the bottom line in the Christian life. If you receive what I'll be sharing with you in the following pages, it'll connect you directly to God. Then He will teach you everything else that you need to know.

The Purpose of Salvation

In John 3:16, Jesus said, *"For God so loved the world, that he gave his only begotten Son, that whosoever believeth in him should not perish, but have everlasting life."*

This is so familiar to people that sometimes, they don't know what it says. But let me tell you what this *doesn't* say. It doesn't say that God so

1

loved the world that He gave His only begotten Son so that if you believed on Him, you would not perish, period. The end goal of salvation is eternal life, not the forgiveness of your sins. It just so happened that in between you and eternal life was a barrier of sin. Sin separated us from relationship with God. So, Jesus came and died for our sins to remove that barrier. What a great gift!

If all you did was come to Jesus to get your sins forgiven so you can go to heaven when you die, but you aren't having a close, intimate, personal relationship with God, you are missing the real purpose of salvation. I know that many people think that's blasphemy because most Christians see the forgiveness of our sins as the goal. It's not. Sin was like an opponent in a sports game that was blocking us from the goal. But what good would it do to remove the goal's defender if we don't take advantage and score?

Am I saying Jesus didn't die for our sins?

No, that's not what I'm saying.

Am I saying that getting our sins forgiven isn't important or necessary?

No. That is absolutely essential, but it is not the end result. The end result of salvation is not to get your sins forgiven; it's to enter into eternal life.

Well, now wait a minute. Isn't eternal life an automatic byproduct of being born again? You go to heaven and live forever with the Lord.

I agree that eternal life includes heaven, but let me just share with you how Scripture describes eternal life. John 3:36 says, *"He that believeth on the Son hath everlasting life."* Everlasting life isn't something that's off in the future; this verse

> The end result of salvation is not to get your sins forgiven; it's to enter into eternal life.

says it's something you can have right now! And it's not just *zoe*, which is the Greek word for a life of joy and peace. It includes that, but it's not limited to that.

What Is Eternal Life?

To get a biblical definition of eternal life, let's go to Jesus, the author of eternal life.

The night before Jesus was crucified, He prayed, *"Father, the hour is come; glorify thy Son, that thy Son also may glorify thee: As thou hast given him power over all flesh, that he should give eternal life to as many as thou hast given him. And this is life eternal, that they might know thee the only true God, and Jesus Christ, whom thou hast sent"* (John 17:1b–3).

Pay special attention to that third verse. Jesus said, *"this is life eternal."* Then He said eternal life is knowing God and Jesus Christ.

You might be disappointed with that definition. You might say, "I already know God. I thought it was something more dynamic than that. I thought it was living forever or something like that."

Well, did you know that everybody lives forever? There is no such thing as a person ceasing to exist. Your spirit man is immortal. It'll live forever either in heaven or in hell.

Well yes, but I was thinking specifically that eternal life is living forever in heaven.

Again, according to John 3:36 and John 6:54, it's something that we can have now.

The key to understanding this is recognizing the Bible uses this word "know" differently than what most of us do today. Genesis 4:1 says, *"And Adam knew Eve his wife; and she conceived"* and bore a son. You have to know a person more than just intellectually in order to have a child. This is talking about an intimate union and communion.

So, when Jesus said, *"And this is life eternal, that they might know thee the only true God, and Jesus Christ, whom thou hast sent"* (John 17:3), this is knowing God in an intimate, personal way. It's much more than just knowledge. It's intimate, personal relationship. It just amazes me to think that God not only wants to forgive us, but He wants intimacy with us. He wants us to experience Him. That's what eternal life is.

Experience Trumps an Argument

The most important encounter I had with the Lord happened on March 23, 1968. I had an experience where I began to know God in an intimate, personal way. I had been born again for a decade, but I got saved as an eight-year-old kid so I wouldn't go to hell. I didn't *know* the Lord in the way Jesus spoke of us having eternal life at that time. But this intimacy with the Lord changed everything.

Years later, I was drafted and sent to Vietnam. While I was there, I remember a man who came to a Bible study I was holding. He listened to me for just a brief period of time, and then he started asking me these really tough questions. He got up, started mocking me, and ridiculed what I was doing. He said, "There is no God. I'm leaving! Who will go with me?"

> It just amazes me to think that God not only wants to forgive us, but He wants intimacy with us.

My entire group left with this atheist! So, I sat there and prayed, "O God, what a mess. Help me to learn so I can answer people's questions and represent You properly."

As I was praying, this man who had ruined my Bible study walked back in, sat down, and made like he was reading a book. Then I prayed, "O God, give me another chance." Then this guy walked over to me and said, "I want what you have." I was shocked! I said, "Why? You just out-argued me. You made a fool of me." He said, "I'm a Princeton graduate. My whole life is built on intellect. I out-argued you, but you've got something that's more than intellect. You've got an experience with God. I want that." And I was able to lead this man to the Lord. It was awesome!

This man saw that I had "eternal life." He saw a relationship and it drew him to the Lord. That's what people are looking for today. It's not about what we know. It's about who we know.

There are historical accounts of Christians in the Colosseum displaying such joy and peace as they were put to death, that Romans would rush into the arena and profess Jesus as their Savior even though it meant their death too. The eternal life that was on display in these Christians' lives was so powerful that people would give their last breath to experience the same thing.

They didn't pass out tracts. They didn't preach and tell the crowd they were going to hell. They just let their love and fellowship with the Lord speak louder than words. Sadly, this is a missing quality in most Christians' lives today.

You may know about God. You may have read the Bible for the purpose of winning an argument or so that you can discuss it with others, but you may not know God. Salvation isn't just knowing some facts about the Bible or acknowledging that He exists. Even the devil does that (James 2:19). You have to connect personally with the Lord. The good news is, God wants this more than you want it!

I can truthfully say I have not plumbed the depths of relationship with God. I still want to know Him more. Yet there have been times when I honestly felt like I was going to explode because I'd been fellowshipping with God and He was so real in my life.

I have experienced God. I know Him—maybe not as much as I should but more than I ever have. Can you say that you know Him intimately? That is what eternal life is all about.

> You have to connect personally with the Lord.

Eternal life is not just for the "sweet by and by," but for the "rough now and now." You can experience it through intimacy with God today. I believe that this will change your life. It's one of the most important things that God has ever shown me.

The Wrong Message

Sad to say, there are a lot of people who are drawn to the Lord for reasons that don't lead to eternal life. Part of it is because, somewhere along the line, the church decided to change the message. If all that is preached is "Come to the Lord to get your sins forgiven so you won't go to hell," then that's all you can have faith for. Faith *only* comes by hearing (Rom. 10:17), and most people have not heard the real message of eternal life. So, many Christians are saved and stuck! They are not living the abundant, full life that God wants them to have. They don't know the Lord on a close, personal level.

> Eternal life is not just for the "sweet by and by," but for the "rough now and now."

I'll admit that your salvation won't be complete until you get to heaven, because you'll get a glorified body and a glorified soul—then you'll know all things, even as you are known (1 Cor. 13:12). But salvation is not about just holding on until you go to heaven, and then experiencing eternal life. God wants you to know Him now. He wants you to feel His pleasure and acceptance totally free of condemnation.

I believe that heaven's going to be a blast. But you can pray, *"Thy kingdom come. Thy will be done in earth, as it is in heaven"* (Matt. 6:10) right now.

You can have heaven in your heart. You can talk to God, and He will talk back to you (John 10:27). You can ask Him questions, and He'll give you answers. You can have a relationship with God that the Bible calls eternal life!

> God wants you to feel His pleasure and acceptance totally free of condemnation.

I'm not the sharpest knife in the drawer. I'm not the most charismatic person. I'm not criticizing myself; I'm just saying that if I was God, I wouldn't have chosen me. Yet He speaks to me, not in an audible voice, but He speaks to me because of this relationship, this eternal life.

Eternal Life Changes Everything

The second most important encounter I ever had with the Lord was on January 31, 2002. God spoke to me through Psalm 78:41 that I had limited Him through my small thinking. When I took the limits off God, it changed everything for our ministry: the number of people we minister to and the amount of financial support we receive. This was as a direct result of eternal life, so I know, from personal experience, that relationship with God is what is missing in people's lives.

In John 14:12, Jesus revealed the potential of a true born-again believer when He said, *"He that believeth on me, the works that I do shall he do also; and greater* works *than these shall he do...."* Now, I haven't arrived, but praise God, I've seen God do great miracles through me, including my own son raised from the dead, my wife raised from the dead, blind eyes opened, and deaf ears opened.

People's lives have been changed. God has supplied finances, and we've had buildings built in order to train other people. It all came to pass out of this relationship.

So many people today don't have any real power. They don't have a peace that passes understanding (Phil. 4:7). They don't have joy that is unspeakable and full of glory (1 Pet. 1:8). There are a lot of Christians who are sick, poor, angry, and bitter. They only know *about* God. He's a distant being to them. Again, if all you do is believe that there's one God, you haven't done anything that the devil hasn't done. He believes and even trembles at the name of God (James 2:19).

In my life, there have been many times when, without relationship with God, I would have caved. But when God Almighty tells you how much He loves you, it just doesn't matter that much what other people think. You may have been rejected.

You may be going through problems in your marriage. You might be having problems with your kids. But eternal life is what you need in order to deal with them. If God tells you that He loves you and He builds you up, which He always will, then even when things aren't going right in the natural, you'll be experiencing eternal life. You might be thinking, *Oh, I could never reach there*. You can!

> If all you do is believe that there's one God, you haven't done anything that the devil hasn't done.

There have been times in my life, as I'm sure there have been with you too, when people have treated me badly. I have been run out of town. I have been kidnapped. I have been threatened to be killed. But in those times, God's presence was so powerful. He'd tell me that He loved me and that He was going to take care of me. Feeling the acceptance of God made it all worth it. You might not know what I'm talking about, but you can have that kind of a relationship with God. Even if everybody forsakes you, you'll know He will never forsake you. You'll be so full that it won't matter whether anybody else appreciates you or not.

I had a man come to me one time, and he just was reading me the riot act telling me how wrong I was. He was probably correct on some of it, but I just stopped him right in the middle of it and said, "Who died and made you God? God loves me. God likes me in spite of my failures. I just don't really care that much about what you say. Compared to God, you're nobody." Maybe I should have been kinder than I was, but that was the way it happened.

> If God tells you that He loves you and He builds you up, which He always will, then even when things aren't going right in the natural, you'll be experiencing eternal life.

My point, though, is when you have relationship with God, it puts other relationships in perspective. It gives you an advantage that people who don't know God don't have. No person who has a relationship with God should ever be at the mercy of a person with an argument. This relationship with God is what the Bible calls eternal life.

I was raised in church, and even though I loved the Lord, my mind hadn't been renewed to the truths I'm sharing with you. I had a desire to tell everybody about the Lord, but the way it had been modeled for me was to basically tell people about hell. So, I went into bars and would pass out tracts that said, "What You Must Do to Go to Hell." On the inside, it was totally blank. When you turned it to the back page, it read, "That's right, you don't have to do anything, because you're already headed to hell, you sinner!" It is true that because of sin, people go to hell, so they do need to repent. Jesus will save them from hell. But that's not what

I should have been emphasizing. The real reason Jesus came was to give them eternal life, which is a present-tense reality.

I'd been taught that God couldn't really love us or fellowship with us, because we were so inferior to Him. It was all about what we could do for Him, so we focused on leading other people to the Lord. We became human doings instead of human beings. God does want us to be the salt and light of this earth (Matt. 5:13–16), but our purpose, the justification for our existence, is to know Him first and then to make Him known to others. Out of that should come changing other people's lives. Every good thing that comes in our lives ought to come from knowing God, or what the Bible calls eternal life.

> The real reason Jesus came was to give them eternal life, which is a present-tense reality.

Better to Be with the Lord

When I was in Vietnam, I remember I went through an experience where I could see the Vietnamese coming up the hill. I could see the muzzle fire from their weapons. People were dying all around me. I could have been fearful, but I was just so in love with the Lord that I was thinking, *O Jesus, this is great! I could see You before the day is over!* The Holy Spirit was just encouraging me, and I actually started praying for the Vietnamese who were charging our position: "Father, if I die, I know where I'm going. But these people don't know You." You may be thinking, *Brother, you're weird*. But I think you're weird.

Paul wrote in Philippians 1:21–24 that he was in a strait between two things. He said he had a desire to depart and be with Christ—which would be far better than staying here on earth—but he knew he needed to stay in order to minister to other people. Paul had this attitude I'm talking about. He also wrote that *"we walk by faith, not by sight"* (2 Cor. 5:7). A little before that, he wrote, *"we look not at the things which are seen, but at the things which are not seen"* (2 Cor. 4:18).

If you are born again, then like Paul and my Vietnam experience, you could be so excited about heaven that if somebody threatened you with death, it'd be all you could do to restrain yourself from hugging and thanking them. To depart and be with Christ is far greater. You're just staying here because you feel that you've got work to do. You can get to that place, but not by just reading about it. You have to experience God. That's what eternal life is.

Luke 24 records the story of the two disciples going up to Emmaus. It says they were sad because they thought Jesus—the one on whom they'd staked their lives, the one who they believed was the

Christ—had died. Then here comes the resurrected Jesus walking beside them. The Scripture says they didn't recognize Him because *"their eyes were holden"* (Luke 24:16). When they did recognize Him, their sadness was gone. All of their fear was gone. They ran back to Jerusalem (Luke 24:32–33) and told the other disciples that Jesus had appeared to them. Everything changed when they realized that He was with them.

> You could be so excited about heaven that if somebody threatened you with death, it'd be all you could do to restrain yourself from hugging and thanking them.

The Effects of Eternal Life: Praise

Let me give you another example of Paul, in Acts 16:9–25. He'd seen a man in a vision saying to come over to Macedonia and help them. It was a vision from God.

So, he and Silas went there and wound up going to Philippi. There, they started seeing people born again. But then Paul cast a demon out of a girl who was using divination, and the people who were making money off of her reported him to the magistrates. They seized him and Silas, beat them to within an inch of their lives, and threw them into prison.

Later, when the Philippian jailer came to rescue them, he had to ask for a light because there was no light in there. So, this was a filthy, stinking, rotten dungeon that I guarantee didn't have good hygiene or sanitation. Their feet were in the stocks, so they couldn't even get comfortable. The average Christian would have been complaining, but look what they did in this situation: *"And at midnight Paul and Silas prayed, and sang praises unto God: and the prisoners heard them"* (Acts 16:25). This is amazing!

When Jesus came into Jerusalem on Palm Sunday, He told the scribes and Pharisees, *"Out of the mouth of babes and sucklings thou hast perfected praise"* (Matt. 21:16). That was a quotation from Psalm 8:2, which says, *"Out of the mouth of babes and sucklings hast thou ordained strength because of thine enemies, that thou mightest still the enemy and the avenger."* So, you see that praise is strength to still the enemy and the avenger. When you've got your back against the wall, one of the greatest things you can do is start praising God.

Second Chronicles 20 shows when invading armies had come against King Jehoshaphat, he set the worshipers in the front, not the warriors. And when they came over a hill, they saw that these enemy armies had wiped each other out. The spoil they left behind was so bountiful that it took three whole days to haul it all. That's powerful!

Some people might say, "Well, the reason Paul and Silas were praising God at midnight was because they were doing spiritual warfare. They were trying to get out of the situation they were in." But they weren't praising God to get something; they were praising God because they really loved Him! They were experiencing eternal life.

> When you've got your back against the wall, one of the greatest things you can do is start praising God.

Counting All Things Loss

In Philippians 3:3, Paul said, *"For we are the circumcision, which worship God in spirit, and rejoice in Christ Jesus, and have no confidence in the flesh."* What a radical statement. Paul wrote, in Galatians 2:20, *"I am crucified with Christ: nevertheless I live; yet not I, but Christ liveth in me: and the life which I now live in the flesh I live by the faith of the Son of God, who loved me, and gave himself for me."* He said he was living out of the spirit. It was actually Christ living through his born-again spirit. It wasn't his own natural ability.

Then, back in Philippians, Paul wrote, *"Though I might also have confidence in the flesh"* (Phil. 3:4a). It'd be one thing for a person who doesn't have very many talents or abilities to say they have no confidence in their flesh, but Paul had it all together. He listed a few of his accomplishments in Philippians 3:5–6, which says, *"Circumcised the eighth day, of the stock of Israel, of the tribe of Benjamin, an Hebrew of the Hebrews; as touching the law, a Pharisee; concerning zeal, persecuting the church; touching the righteousness which is in the law, blameless."*

> There is nothing wrong with personal accomplishments, but you shouldn't value those things more than you value your personal relationship with God.

Some of the accomplishments he listed were absolutely essential to being a Jew. As a Benjamite, he belonged to one of the leading tribes, and he was without peer concerning how strict he was. But then he wrote, *"But what things were gain to me, those I counted loss for Christ. Yea doubtless, and I count all things* but *loss for the excellency of the knowledge of Christ Jesus my Lord: for whom I have suffered the loss of all things, and do count them* but *dung, that I may win Christ"* (Phil. 3:7–8).

This is amazing. If he hadn't come to faith in Jesus, Paul could have been over the Sanhedrin. If he were alive today, he would have had a Doctorate in Divinity. He had everything going for him. You know what most people do with their achievements? They frame them and put them on the wall. Paul said his were like dung. That's powerful! Why did he disesteem all of these things? For *"the excellency of the knowledge of Christ Jesus"* his Lord! There is nothing wrong with personal accomplishments, but you shouldn't value those things more than you value your personal relationship with God.

Paul went on to write, "*And be found in him, not having mine own righteousness, which is of the law, but that which is through the faith of Christ, the righteousness which is of God by faith: That I may know him*" (Phil. 3:9–10a).

In comparison to knowing God, everything else was like dung. Can you say that? This is what the normal Christian life is supposed to be.

Knowing God

One of the reasons that I can minister with nothing but my Bible is because I'm not ministering a lesson that I've learned. I don't have to go get my notes and study them. I live it. I'm just sharing with you things that are a real part of me. It's the whole focus of my life. It's all about knowing God and making Him known. That's eternal life.

When I study the Word, I pray, "Father, I'm believing that You're going to speak to me." One time, after I'd read two or three verses, God showed me something I hadn't seen before. It was scriptures I had read, but I began to see them in a different way. I wound up pushing the Bible back and just meditating on it. Then I remembered that I hadn't finished my daily Bible readings. So, I shelved those thoughts and went back to reading.

After reading a few more verses, I heard the Lord ask, "What are you doing?" I said, "I'm reading the Bible." He asked, "Why?" I said, "So You could speak to me." Then He went silent. After a moment, I got to thinking, *The reason I'm reading the Bible is so God can speak to me. He started speaking, and I basically rejected His voice because it interrupted my Bible reading!* If God speaks to you on the very first verse you've read, forget the rest! It's all about communion with God. It's not about you checking off that you did your daily Bible readings.

I remember that when I first got back from Vietnam; I hadn't had Christian fellowship for nineteen months. I was so excited about being back with my friends. We went to meetings all over the Dallas/Fort Worth Metroplex, and we were out until one o'clock nearly every morning. After a solid month of that, I started to run on empty. I wasn't having as much joy, peace, and fellowship with the Lord as I'd had in Vietnam. So, I prayed, "God, what's wrong?" and He said, "You don't have any time for Me. You're too busy going to church."

Now, the Bible says, don't forsake the assembling of yourselves together (Heb. 10:25), so I wouldn't tell you to quit going to church. But you can't let church or even ministry ruin your relationship with the Lord.

Ministering to the Lord

In Acts 13, there were prophets and teachers gathered, and verse 2 says that *"as they ministered to the Lord, and fasted, the Holy Ghost said, Separate me Barnabas and Saul for the work whereunto I have called them."* Most people just skip over this part about *"ministered to the Lord."* What does it mean to minister to the Lord?

> You can't let church or even ministry ruin your relationship with the Lord.

Scripture says that God inhabits our praises (Ps. 22:3). When we start praising God, He loves it. It's not because He needs us to boost His ego or something. God created us for love. He created us for fellowship.

In Revelation 4:11, it says that God created us for His pleasure. But it says it wasn't just His original purpose; we were and *are* created for His pleasure—present and even future tense! God created us for love. He did not create us just for service. He could have created more angels for that.

> When we start praising God, He loves it.

When you love someone, it hurts if they don't love you back. God is the same way. The Bible says in 1 John 4:8 that He is love. That's not just something that He has; that's who He is. And He longs for you to love Him back.

Blessing the Lord

What does it mean to "bless the Lord"? When I tell the Lord I love Him, I believe that that blesses Him. Psalm 34:1–4 says, *"I will bless the Lord at all times: his praise* shall *continually* be *in my mouth. My soul shall make her boast in the Lord: the humble shall hear* thereof, *and be glad. O magnify the*

> God did not create us just for service. He could have created more angels for that.

Lord with me, and let us exalt his name together. I sought the Lord, and he heard me, and delivered me from all my fears."

How do you bless the Lord? I guarantee, it's not by saying, "Bless You, Lord." When my two sons were younger, I took them out, and we went and played all day long. We rode horses, we made dams in a creek, and we ate junk food. We just had a great day. When we got back home that night, I cleaned them up, and we had our devotions. I turned out the light, and as I was leaving my youngest son's bedroom, he said, "Dad, you are a good dad." Do you know what that did for me? It blessed me! He didn't make the sign of the cross and say in a religious voice, "Bless you, Dad," but him showing his appreciation blessed me. This is what happens when we love the Lord. That's what these people were doing in Acts 13:1–3.

So many of our religious prayers today are all about asking for things or talking about how unworthy we are. But instead of complaining about our sorriness, we ought to praise God for His greatness, that He loves people like us.

Think about Adam and Eve. What was their prayer life like before they sinned? They had all the food they needed. They didn't have clothes to believe for. The climate was perfect. They didn't have a dysfunctional family that raised them. They didn't have anything going on in society. They each had the perfect mate. There were no demons to rebuke. There were no sins to confess. Most Christians wouldn't have any relationship with God if they didn't have all those things to deal with. And yet, they fellowshipped with Him every day, just talking to Him.

> We ought to praise God for His greatness, that He loves people like us.

He inhabited their praises and just enjoyed their presence.

I'm not saying that we don't ask God for things. James 4:2b says, *"Ye have not, because ye ask not."* John 16:24b says, *"Ask, and ye shall receive, that your joy may be full."* There is a place for asking, but the bottom line is, we need to be loving, blessing, and ministering unto God. If we would put the emphasis on knowing Him, on relationship, we'll start experiencing eternal life. God will never let us out-give Him. If we start blessing Him, He's going to bless us back.

Enter Eternal Life with God

You might say, "All right, you've sold me. How do I do it?" Well, you start by telling Him you want to know Him more. Just pray, "Father, reveal Yourself to me." Jesus said, in John 6:63b, *"The words that I speak unto you, they are spirit, and* they *are life.*" You start developing this relationship with Him by looking in His Word! For instance, take Ephesians 1:6, where it says you are *"accepted in the beloved"* and begin to confess it. According to Hebrews 11:6, you are pleasing to God because you've put faith in Jesus. Start speaking these things and blessing God. You will begin entering into eternal life!

> If we would put the emphasis on knowing Him, on relationship, we'll start experiencing eternal life.

Let me go a step further: You may be born again, but you may have never received the baptism of the Holy Spirit, which involves speaking in tongues. The Bible says that when you speak in tongues, it's your spirit praying (1 Cor. 14:14) and that you build yourself up on your most holy faith (Jude 20). It says in Acts 1:8 that *"ye shall receive power, after that the Holy Ghost is come upon you.*" That word "power" is translated from the Greek word *dunamis*. It's where we get the word "dynamo" and "dynamite" from. You have power on the inside of you when you receive the Holy Spirit, and when you speak in tongues, it's just like flipping on a switch. Jesus said that when the Holy Spirit would come, He would lead you into all truth (John 16:13) and bring to your remembrance what Jesus has said (John 14:26). You connect with God the Father and Jesus through the Holy Spirit.

Receive Jesus as Your Savior

Choosing to receive Jesus Christ as your Lord and Savior is the most important decision you'll ever make!

God's Word promises, *"That if thou shalt confess with thy mouth the Lord Jesus, and shalt believe in thine heart that God hath raised him from the dead, thou shalt be saved. For with the heart man believeth unto righteousness; and with the mouth confession is made unto salvation"* (Rom. 10:9–10). *"For whosoever shall call upon the name of the Lord shall be saved"* (Rom. 10:13). By His grace, God has already done everything to provide salvation. Your part is simply to believe and receive.

Pray out loud: "Jesus, I acknowledge that I've sinned and need to receive what you did for the forgiveness of my sins. I confess that You are my Lord and Savior. I believe in my heart that God raised You from the dead. By faith in Your Word, I receive salvation now. Thank You for saving me."

The very moment you commit your life to Jesus Christ, the truth of His Word instantly comes to pass in your spirit. Now that you're born again, there's a brand-new you!

Please contact us and let us know that you've prayed to receive Jesus as your Savior. We'd like to send you some free materials to help you on your new journey. Call our Helpline: **719-635-1111** (available 24 hours a day, seven days a week) to speak to a staff member who is here to help you understand and grow in your new relationship with the Lord.

Welcome to your new life!

Receive the Holy Spirit

As His child, your loving heavenly Father wants to give you the supernatural power you need to live a new life. *"For every one that asketh receiveth; and he that seeketh findeth; and to him that knocketh it shall be opened…how much more shall your heavenly Father give the Holy Spirit to them that ask him?"* (Luke 11:10–13).

All you have to do is ask, believe, and receive! Pray this: "Father, I recognize my need for Your power to live a new life. Please fill me with Your Holy Spirit. By faith, I receive it right now. Thank You for baptizing me. Holy Spirit, You are welcome in my life."

Some syllables from a language you don't recognize will rise up from your heart to your mouth (1 Cor. 14:14). As you speak them out loud by faith, you're releasing God's power from within and building yourself up in the spirit (1 Cor. 14:4).

You can do this whenever and wherever you like.

It doesn't really matter whether you felt anything or not when you prayed to receive the Lord and His Spirit. If you believed in your heart that you received, then God's Word promises you did. *"Therefore I say unto you, What things soever ye desire, when ye pray, believe that ye receive them, and ye shall have them"* (Mark 11:24). God always honors His Word—believe it!

We would like to rejoice with you, pray with you, and answer any questions to help you understand more fully what has taken place in your life!

Please contact us to let us know that you've prayed to be filled with the Holy Spirit and to request the book *The New You & the Holy Spirit*. This book will explain in more detail about the benefits of being filled with the Holy Spirit and speaking in tongues. Call our Helpline: **719-635-1111** (available 24 hours a day, seven days a week).

Call for Prayer

If you need prayer for any reason, you can call our Helpline, 24 hours a day, seven days a week at **719-635-1111**. A trained prayer minister will answer your call and pray with you.

Every day, we receive testimonies of healings and other miracles from our Helpline, and we are ministering God's nearly-too-good-to-be-true message of the Gospel to more people than ever. So, I encourage you to call today!

About the Author

Andrew Wommack's life was forever changed the moment he encountered the supernatural love of God on March 23, 1968. As a renowned Bible teacher and author, Andrew has made it his mission to change the way the world sees God.

Andrew's vision is to go as far and deep with the Gospel as possible. His message goes far through the *Gospel Truth* television program, which is available to over half the world's population. The message goes deep through discipleship at Charis Bible College, headquartered in Woodland Park, Colorado. Founded in 1994, Charis has campuses across the United States and around the globe.

Andrew also has an extensive library of teaching materials in print, audio, and video. More than 200,000 hours of free teachings can be accessed at **awmi.net**.

Contact Information

Andrew Wommack Ministries, Inc.

PO Box 3333
Colorado Springs, CO 80934-3333
info@awmi.net
awmi.net

Helpline: 719-635-1111 (available 24/7)

Charis Bible College

info@charisbiblecollege.org
844-360-9577
CharisBibleCollege.org

For a complete list of all of our offices,
visit **awmi.net/contact-us**.

Connect with us on social media.

Andrew's LIVING COMMENTARY BIBLE SOFTWARE

Andrew Wommack's *Living Commentary* Bible study software is a user-friendly, downloadable program. It's like reading the Bible with Andrew at your side, sharing his revelation with you verse by verse.

Main features:

- Bible study software with a grace-and-faith perspective
- Over 26,000 notes by Andrew on verses from Genesis through Revelation
- *Matthew Henry's Concise Commentary*
- 11 Bible versions
- 2 concordances: *Englishman's Concordance* and *Strong's Concordance*
- 2 dictionaries: *Collaborative International Dictionary* and *Holman's Dictionary*
- Atlas with biblical maps
- Bible and *Living Commentary* statistics
- Quick navigation, including history of verses
- Robust search capabilities (for the Bible and Andrew's notes)
- "Living" (i.e., constantly updated and expanding)
- Ability to create personal notes

Whether you're new to studying the Bible or a seasoned Bible scholar, you'll gain a deeper revelation of the Word from a grace-and-faith perspective.

Purchase Andrew's *Living Commentary* today at **awmi.net/living**, and grow in the Word with Andrew.

Item code: 8350

ANDREW
WOMMACK
MINISTRIES